b1099

577-16

GRAPHIC SCIENCE

THE WORLD OF

FOOD CHAINS

WITH MAX AXIOM SUPER SCIENTIST

Liam O'Donnell

illustrated by Cynthia Martin and Bill Anderson

Raintree

www.raintreepublishers.co.uk
Visit our website to find out
more information about
Raintree books.

To order:
☎ Phone +44 (0) 1865 888066
▤ Fax +44 (0) 1865 314091
▤ Visit www.raintreepublishers.co.uk

Raintree is an imprint of Capstone Global Library Limited, a company incorporated in England and
Wales having its registered office at 7 Pilgrim Street, London EC4V 6LB
Registered company number: 6695882

"Raintree" is a registered trademark of Pearson Education Limited, under licence to Capstone Global
Library Limited

Text © Capstone Press 2008
First published by Capstone Press in 2008
First published in hardback in the United Kingdom by Capstone Global Library in 2010
The moral rights of the proprietor have been asserted.

ISBN 978 1 406 21466 6 (hardback)
14 13 12 11 10

British Library Cataloguing in Publication Data
O'Donnell, Liam, 1970-
Food chains. -- (Graphic science)
577.1'6-dc22
A full catalogue record for this book is available from the British Library.

Art Director and Designer: Bob Lentz
Cover Artist: Tod Smith
Colourist: Krista Ward
UK Editor: Diyan Leake
UK Production: Alison Parsons
Originated by Capstone Global Library
Printed and bound in China by South China Printing Company Limited

Acknowledgements
The publisher would like to thank the following for permission to reproduce copyright material:
Corbis p. 25 (Eric and David Hosking); iStockphoto Inc. p. 10 (Sandra vom Stein); Minden Pictures
p. 17 (D.P. Wilson/FLPA); Shutterstock p. 11 (Roux Frederic)

CONTENTS

Super Scientist Max Axiom stops at a local outdoor market before an amazing journey into the world of food chains.

Mmmmm.

This apple will satisfy my hunger.

CRRUNCHH!

Just grabbing a quick snack to give me energy for the ride.

You know, all food has energy inside.

Every time we eat a snack or a meal, our bodies absorb proteins, minerals, and vitamins.

5

Every ecosystem on earth contains many food chains.

In most cases, all the energy comes from a single source.

The sun!

But most living things can't absorb this energy directly.

Plants have an amazing ability to turn the sun's energy into food.

DEFINITION

Photosynthesis a chemical process by which green plants make their food. Plants use energy from the sun to turn water and carbon dioxide into food, and they give off oxygen as a by-product.

This chemical process is called photosynthesis.

The next link in a food chain leads to a consumer.

Consumers are plants and animals that eat other organisms for energy.

In this food chain, the grasshopper is the primary consumer.

It's the first organism in the chain to eat.

MMUNNCH

By munching on leaves, a grasshopper absorbs the plant's stored energy.

BOINGG!

It uses this energy to grow, reproduce . . .

BOINGG!

. . . and, of course, hop!

BOINGG!

Plants are the only producers in a food chain, but there are three types of consumers.

Many scientists believe the largest animals to ever walk the earth were herbivores. Measuring 37 metres (123 feet) long and weighing more than 90 tonnes (100 tons), the *Argentinasaurus* ate a lot of plants, including entire evergreen trees!

Consumers such as grasshoppers, which only eat plants, are called herbivores.

MUNCH
MUNCH

But other consumers have an appetite for another type of meal.

SQUEEACK!!

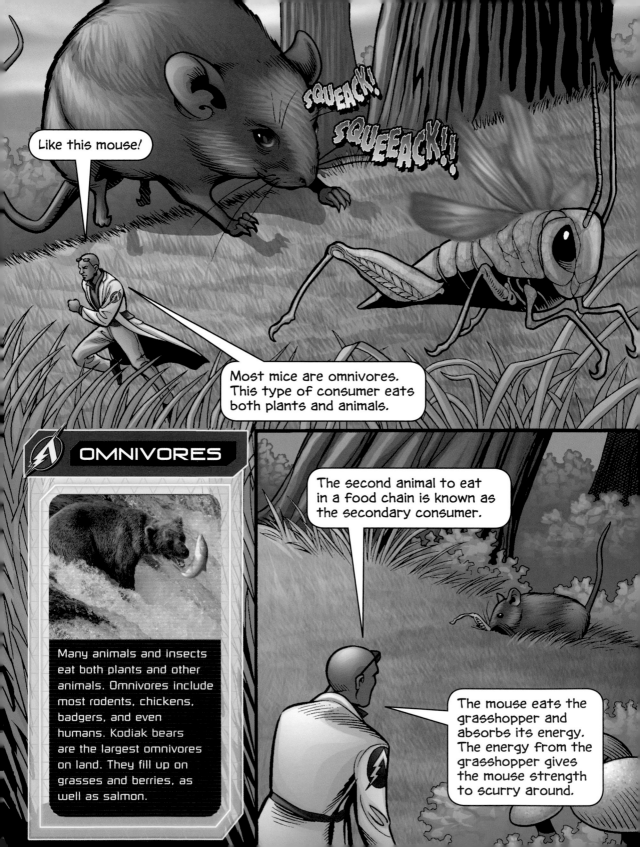

We've learned how food chains connect all living things together.

In this food chain, the hawk is known as the top predator.

Top predators are not threatened or eaten by any other animals in their community.

Does this make them the final link in the chain?

To find out, we have to go off road!

DID YOU KNOW?

Humans are one of the world's top predators. People have no natural predators. And since we eat a variety of foods, we're at the top of many food chains.

In the deepest, darkest corners of every ecosystem lurks a group of organisms called decomposers.

These creepy-crawly creatures are the final link in every food chain.

DECOMPOSERS

Many remain hidden from other forest dwellers, ready to feed on dead plant and animal parts.

But there's no reason to fear decomposers. They're always in action right under our feet.

Slugs, worms, and fungi are all decomposers.

And they all help break down dead plants and animals into nutrients.

Every ecosystem has many food chains. Often, they overlap and connect into a system called a web.

And no one knows food webs better than my old science teacher, Mrs. Breem.

Hey, Mrs B! How's the world of science?

Maxwell! My, you've grown. You must have learned to eat your vegetables.

Actually, that's kind of the reason I'm here. I heard your class was studying food webs.

Yes, this is Keira. She's studying the food web of the park.

Hello, Mr Axiom!

18

Humans are sometimes responsible for putting a food chain at risk.

Some farms use chemicals to help their crops grow and stay healthy. These chemicals are called pesticides.

Pesticides are too small to see, but they can be very harmful to people and animals.

Pesticides can wash from the farmer's soil into nearby rivers.

Even the fastest birds on earth couldn't escape the impact of pesticides. In the late 1950s, the number of peregrine falcons in the United Kingdom dropped dramatically. Scientists discovered that peregrines were consuming birds that had eaten insects contaminated with DDT. This pesticide had travelled up the food chain to the top predator. The DDT caused peregrine falcon eggs to thin and break before young could develop. Soon, the falcons were an endangered species. Restrictions on DDT helped the birds make a comeback but there are still not very many in southeast and east England, and their numbers are going down again in northern Scotland.

The harmful chemicals are absorbed by producers.

Then, they are transferred from one animal to the next through the food chain.

Pesticides can kill the animals or make them sick.

25

MORE ABOUT FOOD CHAINS

*An animal's mouth often determines its choice of foods. For example, some whales have strong teeth for eating large fish and seals. Other whales, such as the blue whale, have no teeth at all. These gigantic mammals strain tiny organisms through a comblike series of plates, which hang from their upper jaw.

*Some animals eat only one type of food every day! Koalas in Australia eat nothing but eucalyptus leaves. The koala's picky diet makes their habitat extremely fragile. If eucalyptus trees suddenly disappeared, koalas would have no other food to eat.

*Many consumers have amazing abilities and features for capturing their prey. Cheetahs sprint 113 kilometres (70 miles) per hour to snag a rabbit or an antelope. Common loons dive more than 76 metres (250 feet) underwater in search of small fish or leeches. Some spiders make webs that are strong enough to capture birds.

*Scavengers are another important part of food chains and food webs. These animals eat the leftover portions of dead animals. Their bodies break down these larger chunks into smaller bits, which decomposers can then return to the soil.

*A parasite is an animal or plant that needs to live on or inside another animal or plant to survive. Parasites aren't usually listed on food chains or food webs. But even top predators can't escape these greedy creatures. Leeches are a parasite that will latch onto animals or humans for a tasty meal of blood.

 Carnivores don't have to be large meat-eaters such as lions or sharks. Plants can be carnivores as well. Venus flytraps, pitcher plants, and other carnivorous plants live where there are not many nutrients in the soil. These types of plants get food by capturing small prey in their traps.

 Wash what you eat! Farmers often spray vegetables and fruits with pesticides. These chemicals keep pests away in the field but can be harmful to people and animals. Rinsing produce before eating helps eliminate any remaining pesticides and reduces the chance of getting sick.

MORE ABOUT

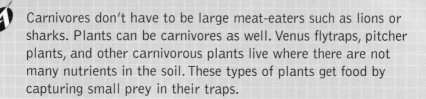

Super Scientist

Real name: Maxwell Axiom
Height: 1.86 m (6 ft 1 in.)
Weight: 87 kg (13 st. 10 lb.)
Eyes: Brown   Hair: None

Super capabilities: Super intelligence; able to shrink to the size of an atom; sunglasses give X-ray vision; lab coat allows for travel through time and space.

Origin: Since birth, Max Axiom seemed destined for greatness. His mother, a marine biologist, taught her son about the mysteries of the sea. His father, a nuclear physicist and volunteer park warden, showed Max the wonders of the earth and sky.

One day, while Max was hiking in the hills, a megacharged lightning bolt struck him with blinding fury. When he awoke, he discovered a new-found energy and set out to learn as much about science as possible. He travelled the globe studying every aspect of the subject. Then he was ready to share his knowledge and new identity with the world. He had become Max Axiom, Super Scientist.

GLOSSARY

carnivore animal that eats only meat

ecosystem community of animals and plants interacting with their environment

fungi organisms that have no leaves, flowers, or roots. Mushrooms and moulds are fungi.

herbivore animal that eats only plants

nutrient substance needed by a living thing to stay healthy

omnivore animal that eats both plants and other animals

organic uses only natural products and no chemicals or pesticides

organism a living plant or animal

pesticide chemical used to kill insects and other pests that eat crops

predator animal that hunts other animals for food

prey animal that is hunted by other animals for food

tertiary of third rank, importance, or value

FIND OUT MORE

Books

Food Chains series (Heinemann Library, 2010)

Food Chains and Webs (Science Answers series), Louise and Richard Spilsbury (Heinemann Library, 2005)

Shark Snacks, Louise and Richard Spilsbury (Raintree, 2005)

Websites

www.bbc.co.uk/schools/ks2bitesize
Click on "Science" and then "Living Things" for an activity and quiz on food chains.

http://www.woodlands-junior.kent.sch.uk/Homework/fooodchains.htm
Log on to this website to see one school's pages on food chains. It also provides links to other websites and online activities on food chains.

INDEX